ACKNOWLEDGEMENTS

Without the assistance of Pepperdine University, this book would not have been published.

Without a grant from the Carlson Family Foundation, and trustee Elaine Boylen, this book would not have been printed.

Without the creative eye of my friend and designer, Jean-Marc Durviaux, this book would not have been so beautiful.

Without my dear wife's encouragement, this book would not have been completed.

And without the intriguing and photogenic community of Malibu, this book would not have even begun.

Thanks to all!

Published by Burton Weiss Publishing

Under the auspices of Creative Storytellers NL, Amsterdam, The Netherlands

Print production by bigger dot (www.biggerdot.com)

Printed in South Korea

ISBN-13: 978-0-9824872-3-5

An electronic version of this book is also available at: www.CreativeStorytellers.com/to-malibu-with-love

ISBN-13: 978-0-9824872-3-5

To Malibu with Love

Maybe it was those Beach Blanket movies or a long-forgotten (except by me) TV series called "Malibu Run" or the fact that I was brought up in the Midwest, where the nearest bodies of water were dingy quarries and muddy rivers…but when my wife and I were transferred to Southern California at the end of 1965, we were determined to live on the beach in that world-famous paradise called Malibu!

And we've lived here ever since. As a matter of fact, we can't think of a place on earth we'd rather be.

Even though it's become a chamber-of-commerce cliché, I still love having the beach at our front door and the mountains at our back door. I love the oak-studded canyons, where horses run and deer still roam. I love watching dolphins leap just 50 feet off the shore, whales pass the tip of Point Dume, and sea lions sun their shiny fur on the rocks. I love the hiking trails with their hidden waterfalls and majestic views. I love the wave-sculpted caves and coves at beaches like Leo Carillo and El Matador. I love the estuaries, where marvelous, long-legged water birds find refuge. I love misty mornings, cloudless autumn days, and sun shafts beaming through a dark, cumulus sky after a winter storm. I love driving the winding canyon roads and riding my bike up PCH and jogging on wet sand. I love body surfing and diving the kelp beds. I love driftwood and shiny pebbles sculpted by the sea. I love sending Christmas cards back east with photos of family members wearing short sleeves to show off winter tans.

Perfect? No. What is? But perhaps this is as close as a world populated by humans can get.

And so I have put together this photographic love letter…to a piece of land and a state of mind that occupy a very special place in my heart.

To you,
Malibu.

With Love,
Buddy Weiss

Only in MALIBU

One morning, while riding my bike along the Zuma Beach parking access road, watching the morning joggers and dog walkers, I ran across an elephant. Yes, a full-grown Indian elephant with floppy ears and a long trunk. On the beach! Fortunately I had my cell phone, so I called my wife. "Quick Karen, grab my camera and get down here. You're not going to believe this!" She did. And I got the shot.

Funny thing is…although this incident seems quite unusual, it's not for Malibu. Keeping to the beach scene, I've marveled at people walking their pet goats, pet llamas, and pet snakes at various times. And just recently I spied a group of ninjas in full regalia battling with fighting sticks.

Malibu is, well, unique. For instance, where else can you see the sun both rise and set over the Pacific? Point Dume is a great place to observe both, by the way.

You see things here you see nowhere else. Like mega movie stars grocery shopping in worn-out mukluks and torn Ts. Another Ralphs shopper who loads up his pack horse instead of his SUV. And one man's private golf course built on coastal land worth more than some small countries.

It's full of surprises. Like our local motion picture theatre. In a community populated with studio moguls, you'd think our local movie house would have a screen larger than your average plasma TV. And the plaque near Cross Creek honoring Malibu Joe. What other community pays homage to its homeless?

As I said…only in Malibu.

Left:

Wearing Trunks at the Beach

Zuma

Left:

Hang 20
Zuma Beach

Right:

Attack of the Ninjas
Westward Beach

Left:

Horseplay
Trancas Beach

Right:

In the Key of Sea
Zuma Beach

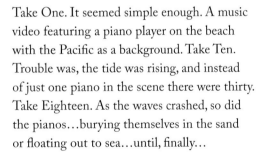

Take One. It seemed simple enough. A music video featuring a piano player on the beach with the Pacific as a background. Take Ten. Trouble was, the tide was rising, and instead of just one piano in the scene there were thirty. Take Eighteen. As the waves crashed, so did the pianos…burying themselves in the sand or floating out to sea…until, finally…

Take Twenty Nine. The pianist himself was no longer on the beach, but waist-deep in the ocean. That's a wrap!

Left:

Horse Power meets Horsepower
Civic Center

Right:

Red, White & Bu
Pepperdine University

3000 for 9-11
Pepperdine University

Where else does the sun both rise...

Looking East from Point Dume

and set over the Pacific?

Looking West from Pepperdine University

MALIBU
is
Wild Country

Mention Malibu to most people and they think strictly of what lies west of PCH. The beach and the ocean. But east of PCH is a whole other world…of cliffs and mountains and canyons. Hiking paths that meander through oak-covered, sun-dappled hills. Hidden streams and, surprisingly, more than a dozen waterfalls beckoning those with a thirst for adventure. Fire roads and single tracks that lure mountain bikers with a siren song. Winding "sports-car" roads that zig through miles of untouched wilderness. Wildflowers that bloom the year around. Ranches where horses and riders can gallop over trails cut through fragrant sage.

Go east, young man! And see the wild side of Malibu.

Left:

Window to Heaven

Castro Crest

Left:

Dunescape
Pacific Coast Highway

Rock Cod
Mulholland Highway

Right:

View From The Top
Castro Crest

Left:

Above the Clouds
Piuma Rd.

Right:

Falling in Love
Lower Escondido Falls

Taking The Plunge
Upper Escondido Falls

Left:

Black Forest

Malibu Creek State Park

Balancing Act

Mishe Mokwa Trail

Echo Canyon-yon-yon

Mishe Mokwa Trail

Right:

Golden Hour

Yerba Buena

Left:

See The Light
Pepperdine University

From Rock, Life
Castro Crest

Right:

Pooled Assets
The Rock Pool, Malibu Creek State Park

MALIBU
is
Wild Flowers

Not too far from my house is a hillside that blazes with golden coreopsis each spring. It's becoming an endangered plant species other places, but here it thrives.

Nature has blessed Malibu with a wealth of year-round, natural beauty. Cattails and pampas grass along the wetlands; holly and lupine in the canyons; black walnut, wild oats and white bells in the canyons.

Man hasn't done such a bad job either. The landscaping here seems more natural, less pretentious than in many other communities. And knowing the community, I think it will stay that way.

Left:

Goldfield
*Giant Coreopsis, Point
Dume Natural Reserve*

Left:

Glorious

Morning Glory,
Pacific Coast Highway

Purple Passion
Periwinkle, Escondido Canyon

Lone Lupine
Escondido Canyon

Right:

Petal Power

Wild Rose, Trancas Canyon

24

Left:

Golden Glow
Spanish Broome, Kanan Road

Right:

Grand Opening
Hummingbird Sage, The Grotto Trail

Glorious Allred
Lance–Leaf Live–Forever, Mishe Mokwa Trail

Left:

Thistle Do It!
Reagan Ranch

Eye-Poppin' Poppies
Point Dume Natural Reserve

Right:

Heavy on the Mustard
Pacific Coast Highway

Left:

Right:

Crown Jewels

Cup of Gold

Crown Daisies, Point Dume

Yellow Mariposa Lily, Sandstone Peak

Bloomin' Great!

Wooly Blue Curl, Mishe Mokwa Trail

Splendor in the Grass

Peninsular Onion, Mishe Mokwa Trail

MALIBU
is
Wild Life

Growing in my front yard are four tall fan palms. And living in those trees is a flock of green parrots. Every morning about 6:30 they suddenly depart to find food or whatever parrots do. And every evening just before the sun sets they return to squabble over who gets what leaf and retire for the night. They're certainly not native, but they're now legal residents and seem quite happy. And I'm happy to have them. With only 13,000 humans scattered over 80 square miles, Malibu is a true nirvana for wildlife.

Gaze out to sea and you'll discover migrating gray whales, schools of dolphin and flocks of pelicans skimming the wave tops. Look to the rocky shoreline for a glimpse of sunbathing sea lions and scurrying crabs. Dive beneath the ocean's surface to view garish garibaldi, bashful bass, elusive octopus and meandering sand sharks. And explore the tide pools for brilliant starfish, purple sea urchins and bright green anemone.

Near The Colony lies a hidden wetland, alive with snowy egrets, blue herons and sharp-eyed hawks.

As evening nears, look to the hills for grazing herds of mule deer. (By the way, you need look no further than Pepperdine to find them.) Then, as night closes in, listen for the plaintive calls of the coyotes, the lonesome hoots of the owls and the echoing screech of Point Dume's resident peafowl.

Red fox still scurry from hiding place to hiding place. Shy bobcats still make appearances in the hills. And mountain lion sightings, although rare, still occur.

Left:

Left:

Malibu Swim Team
Dolphins, Westward Beach

Right:

Jumping for Joy
Zuma Beach

Dolphin Dance
Zuma Beach

Left:

Gray Matter
Gray Whale, Point Dume Headlands

Right:

Madonna
Gray Whale Cow & Calf, Point Dume Headlands

Left:

Like Father, Like Son

Sealions, Westward Beach

Right:

Malibu Rock Singer

Sealion, Point Dume

Sittin' By the

Dock 'o the Bay

Pelicans, Malibu Colony

Above:

Soaring

Pelican, Westward Beach

Right:

Follow the Leader

Pelicans, Point Dume

Left:

Malibu Snow

Snowy Egret, Malibu Creek Wetlands

Right:

White Flite

Great Egret, Little Dume

Left:

Beak to Beak
Great Egret Mother & Chick
Cross Creek Center

Seafood Sampler
Snowy Egret, Little Dume

Right:

Four for Dinner
Snowy Egrets, Riviera II

Left:

Honk if You Love Malibu
Canada Goose, Malibu Creek State Park

Surf Watch
Cormorants, Leo Carillo Beach

Right:

Fly Like the Wind
Osprey, Riviera II

Left:

Swan Lake (What else?)
Lake Malibou

Right:

Buried Treasure
Willet, Zuma Beach

Gotcha!

Left:

Heads Up
Mallard Ducks, Zuma Creek

Cleared for Takeoff
Mallard Ducks, Zuma Creek

Right:

Marsh-Mallard
Rock Pool, Malibu Creek State Park

Left:

Natural Redhead
Red Tailed Hawk, Malibu Creek State Park

Controversial Cock
Point Dume

Right:

Rush Hour
Green Parrots, Pt. Dume

Bird of Paradise
Point Dume

Left:

Nya Nya!
Mule Deer, Pepperdine University

Right:

I'm Outa Here!
Mule Deer, Pepperdine University

Girls' Night Out
Mule Deer, Hughes Research Laboratory

Left:

Coy Coyote

Right:

I'm All Ears
Malibu Creek State Park

Royal Roost
Pelican & Cormorants, El Matador State Beach

MALIBU
is
Wild Times

I woke up early this morning, because I wanted to take a run on the beach with my dog before work. My wife was already dressed for tennis and was packing a change of clothes for her late-morning pilates workout. Typical Malibu.

If one becomes a couch potato in this community, it's one's own fault…for Malibu is a Mecca for adventures and activities. Swimming, hiking, biking and motorcycling. Jogging, fishing, sailing, kayaking. Horseback riding, rock climbing, hang gliding, scuba diving.

Blah blah blah, the list goes on. Boredom is something you really have to work at!

The photographs I've included here are some of my favorites —people doing "their thing" in Malibu.

Left:

Over the Top
Point Dume

Left:

Bar Hopping Malibu Style
Trancas Riders and Ropers

Malibu Air Force

Right:

Getting High on Pt. Dume

Left:

Tri-Cycles
Malibu Triathlon

Hog Heaven
The Rock Store, Mulholland Highway

Right:

Casting Call
Westward Beach

Two Over Easy
Riviera II

MALIBU
is the
Wild West

You can't get much more West than Malibu without swimming. But our heritage is that of the Wild West…as in cowboys and Indians.

The original residents were native Americans – the Chumash tribe. Evidence of their culture can still be found throughout Malibu today.

In the 1800s Malibu was a large rancho owned by one Jose Bartoloe Tapia, for whom Tapia Park is named.

The 1900s saw Malibu used as the location for many western movies. Paramount Studios' western town - with its jail, hotel, bar and dirt streets - still stands, although it's now owned and maintained by the National Park Service. Gary Cooper, Joel McCrea, and Randolph Scott are three of the many stars who drew their six guns here.

Even today, our mountains are dotted with ranches and real cowboys, who still ride horses when they're not driving their 4x4s. Native Americans hold a yearly pow wow at Bluff Park. And, of course, we still have a sheriff.

Left:

Feathers and Fur

Bluff Park

Left:

Pow WOW! Indian Mask
Bluff Park

Right:

Tatavian
Chumash Day Host

Northern Traditional Dancer
Bluff Park

Left:

Malibu 1700
Chumash Hogun

Right:

Malibu Art Fest, Circa: 1450 a.d.
Chumash Cave Paintings

Left:

Howdy Stranger
Cross Creek

Right:

Sticking Your Neck Out
Cross Creek

MALIBU
is wild about
Movies

It's hard to find a day when someone's not shooting a movie, a series, a commercial, a something in Malibu. Been that way since the days when cameras were cranked by hand. But why not? With the sea, the mountains, movie ranches, an old western town, beautiful homes, scenic roads…all close to Hollywood (and its new home in Santa Monica), it just makes sense. As they say, location, location, location!

Left:

Gary Cooper Rode Here
Paramount Ranch

Left:

Hanging Out at Zuma

Right:

Outsourced to Malibu
Westward Beach

Left:

Ambulance in Need of an Ambulance
Mash TV Location

Right:

From MASH to Ash

This spot used to be the location where they filmed MASH. Today it's marked only by this burned-out jeep and ambulance, the legacy of one of our ubiquitous wildfires. But it's fun to stand there looking at the mountains in the background and try to recall…"Isn't that where the hospital tent stood?" Or "I remember Hawkeye napping under that tree."

Above all
MALIBU
is the
Wild Sea

It's mesmerizing. The ocean, that is. That hypnotic sound of waves crashing and receding, crashing and receding just seems to wash away all cares and pressures that life heaps upon us. Perhaps our ancestors indeed did come from the sea, and this is what remains of that ancient heritage. All I know is we humans are drawn to the shore…to watch, to listen, to immerse ourselves in its beauty and tranquility.

Here in Malibu we have 27 miles of breathtaking shoreline, to enjoy. And I've captured a few of them on film and most recently digital sensors. I hope viewing these wet & wild photographs makes you as happy as taking them made me.

Left:

Crashing!
Leo Carillo Beach

Left:

Pilings in Paradise. Cove, that is.

Right:

Weathered and Wonderful
Paradise Cove

Left:

Hope
El Matador State Beach

Tunnel Vision
Leo Carillo Beach

Right:

Water Colors
Riviera I

Left:

Beauty and the Beach
Riviera I

Right:

Sculpted by the Sea
Riviera I

Sunset Para-Surf
Zuma Beach

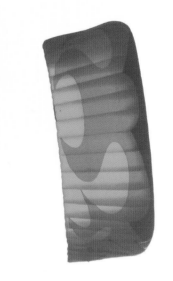

Even in Paradise all is not Perfect

Sure, this book is a love story. But even love stories have their conflicts, their problems, their villains, their seamy sides. And so it is with Malibu.

When I remove my rose-colored glasses, I see the catastrophic wildfires and the unstoppable mudslides. I see the storm-tossed waves that too often ravage the shore and the homes that sit too close upon it. I wade in water that is sometimes impure. I drive over roads buckling from underground pressures. I get stuck in interminable traffic. I hear the arguments over buildings, ball fields, medical facilities and resident services…arguments that never seem to get resolved.

Imperfect? You bet! But perhaps it just makes us appreciate the good in Malibu even more.

Left:

The Telephone-Pole Forest

Pacific Coast Highway

Left:

Whoops!
Point Dume

Tourist Attraction

Right:

No Joy in Mudville
Pacific Coast Highway

Legacy of the Flame
La Costa

Welcome to the
Capital
of
Surfing

Me, I've never been on a surfboard. Boogie boarding and bodysurfing are just fine. But for those whose web feet seem permanently attached to a long board, Malibu is heaven on earth.

From Topanga to County Line the surf is populated with bobbing, wet-suit-clad bodies waiting to catch "the perfect wave." Surfing, in fact, has become almost a symbol for Malibu. I've even had tradesmen leave our house in the middle of a repair job because…the surf's up.

But the center of it all…the Capital of surfing on the mainland…is Surfrider Beach, a stretch of golden sand made famous in Beach Blanket movies and Beach Boys songs from the '50s and '60s. Is that you, Annette?

Standing on a board, knees bent, arms moving for balance isn't the only way to surf either. The waves are now populated by kayakers, sailboarders and parasurfers as well. It's getting so crowded out there you almost need to take a number.

Hey dude, let's see some pictures.

Left:

On Top of the World
Little Dume

Left:

**Home of The Beach Boys,
Gidget and The Big Kahuna**
Riviera II

Right:

Wet & Wild
Little Dume

Face Man
Little Dume

Left:

Multispecies Surfing
Zuma Beach

Right:

Let's Boogie
Zuma Beach

Left:

Sit 'n Surf

Little Dume

Soar 'n Surf

Zuma Beach

Right:

Share 'n Surf

Riviera II

Paddle 'n Surf

Riviera II

Left:

Kite 'n Surf
Broad Beach

Sail 'n Surf
Leo Carillo Beach

Right:

The Last Surfer
Malibu Pier

MALIBU'S
Beauty Shines even when the
Sun Doesn't

I'm sure the Chamber of Commerce would love you to believe it's always sunny in Malibu. But some of our most beautiful days are those when the fog and the mist and the clouds and the overcast have bid the sun goodbye.

Fog gives Malibu a delicious solitude you rarely experience. Rain brings forth breathtaking clouds that tower thousands of feet into the sky. Those brilliant shafts of light that appear upon the ocean when a storm is breaking are beyond belief. And the air after a storm has passed is as clear as crystal.

And then, of course, there's the night…when darkness replaces sunlight and Malibu shimmers with a whole new kind of beauty.

Sun, rain, fog, clouds. In Malibu they're all Chamber of Commerce weather.

Left:

Shafts Upon the Sea
Point Dume

Left:

Rhapsody in Blue
Topanga Beach

Three Swings - No Waiting
Zuma Beach

Right:

Double Vision
Point Dume

Spin Zone
Water Spout off Pt. Dume

Left:

Misty Morning
Point Dume

Night Light
Point Dume

Right:

It's Pier Pleasure!
Malibu Fishing Pier

Sunsets
don't get any
Better

Ooh! Aah! Wow! Those unbelievable Malibu sunsets.

They come in golds, oranges, reds and purples. They appear over the ocean and the mountains. They occur during every season of the year. And just as they happen at the end of the day, I have also placed them at the end of this book.

Enjoy!

Left:

Gasp!
El Matador State Beach

Left:

Ooh!
Point Dume

Right:

Aah!
El Matador State Beach

Yeah!
Point Dume

Left:

Wow!
Point Dume

Amazing
Sycamore Park

Right:

Awesome!
County Line

Holy Moly!
El Matador State Beach